Let's Read About Insects

BEES

by Susan Ashley

Reading consultant: Susan Nations, M.Ed., author/literacy coach/consultant

WEEKLY WR READER®
EARLY LEARNING LIBRARY

Please visit our web site at: www.earlyliteracy.cc
For a free color catalog describing Weekly Reader® Early Learning Library's
list of high-quality books, call 1-877-445-5824 (USA) or 1-800-387-3178 (Canada).
Weekly Reader® Early Learning Library's fax: (414) 336-0164.

Library of Congress Cataloging-in-Publication Data

Ashley, Susan.
     Bees / by Susan Ashley.
        p. cm. — (Let's read about insects)
     Summary: Brief text discusses the life cycle, behavior, and physical characteristics
of bees and describes how honeybees live in colonies and make honey.
     Includes bibliographical references and index.
     ISBN 0-8368-4051-8 (lib. bdg.)
     ISBN 0-8368-4058-5 (softcover)
     1. Bees—Juvenile literature. 2. Honeybee—Juvenile literature.
(1. Bees. 2. Honeybee.) I. Title.
QL565.2.A74   2004
595.79'9—dc22   2003062195

This edition first published in 2004 by
Weekly Reader® Early Learning Library
330 West Olive Street, Suite 100
Milwaukee, WI 53212 USA

Editor: JoAnn Early Macken
Picture research: Diane Laska-Swanke
Art direction and page layout: Tammy Gruenewald

Picture credits: Cover © Brian Kenney; title, p. 5 © Diane Laska-Swanke; p. 7
© Bill Beatty/Visuals Unlimited; pp. 9, 11, 13, 17 © Robert & Linda Mitchell; pp. 15, 19
© E. S. Ross/Visuals Unlimited; p. 21 © Scott Camazine

Printed in the United States of America

1 2 3 4 5 6 7 8 9 08 07 06 05 04

Note to Educators and Parents

Reading is such an exciting adventure for young children! They are beginning to integrate their oral language skills with written language. To encourage children along the path to early literacy, books must be colorful, engaging, and interesting; they should invite the young reader to explore both the print and the pictures.

Let's Read About Insects is a new series designed to help children read about insect characteristics, life cycles, and communities. In each book, young readers will learn interesting facts about the featured insects and how they live.

Each book is specially designed to support the young reader in the reading process. The familiar topics are appealing to young children and invite them to read — and reread — again and again. The full-color photographs and enhanced text further support the student during the reading process.

In addition to serving as wonderful picture books in schools, libraries, homes, and other places where children learn to love reading, these books are specifically intended to be read within an instructional guided reading group. This small group setting allows beginning readers to work with a fluent adult model as they make meaning from the text. After children develop fluency with the text and content, the book can be read independently. Children and adults alike will find these books supportive, engaging, and fun!

— Susan Nations, M.Ed., author, literacy coach,
and consultant in literacy development

Buzz is the sound a bee makes as it flies. It flies from flower to flower. The sound comes from the bee's wings. They move very quickly.

To a bee, a flower is like a grocery store. Bees go to a flower to find food. They collect the pollen. They feed it to young bees. They use the flower's nectar to make honey.

Bees are insects. Like all insects, a bee has six legs. Its body has a head, a thorax, and an abdomen. A bee's body looks fuzzy. It is covered with tiny hairs.

abdomen

head

thorax

9

Honeybees live in large groups. A group is called a **colony**.
A colony has one queen bee. A colony has hundreds of male bees, or drones. It has thousands of female worker bees.

Each bee has a job to do. Drones mate with the queen. The queen spends her life laying eggs. Worker bees raise the young. They gather food and guard the colony.

The bees live in a **hive**. Inside the hive, worker bees build tiny wax rooms. The rooms are called **cells**. The bees store food in some cells. In other cells, they raise young bees.

cells

A bee begins life as an egg. The queen bee lays an egg in a cell. When it hatches, it becomes a larva. A larva looks like a small worm.

eggs

After a few days,
the larva changes
shape. It becomes
a pupa. Soon the
pupa becomes a
young bee.

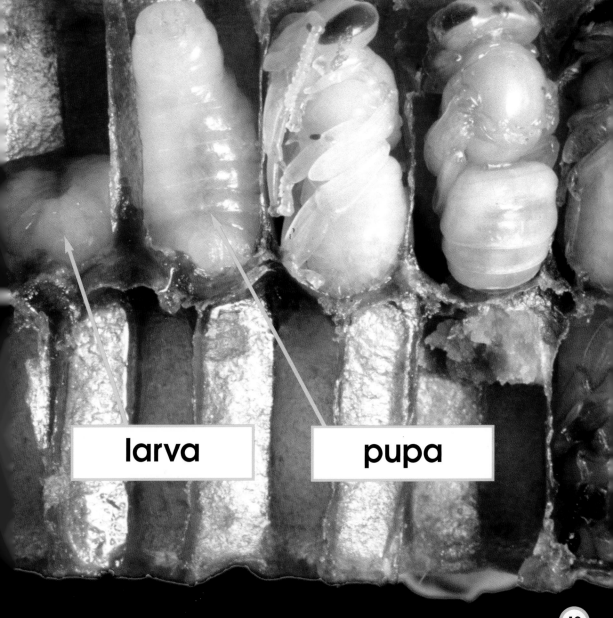

larva

pupa

A young bee is put
to work right away.
It cleans its cell.
The queen can lay
a new egg there.
Then another young
bee joins the hive.

Glossary

abdomen — the back part of an insect's body

cells — wax rooms inside a beehive

colony — a group that lives together

nectar — a sweet liquid from plants that bees make into honey

thorax — the middle part of an insect's body

For More Information

Books

Micucci, Charles. *The Life and Times of the Honeybee.* Boston: Houghton Mifflin, 1997.

Pascoe, Elaine. *Insects Visit Flowers.* Milwaukee: Gareth Stevens, 2000.

Schaefer, Lola. *Honey Bees and Flowers.* Mankato, Minn.: Pebble Books, 2000.

Web Sites

Honey for Kids
honey.com/kids/
Facts and games about honeybees

Index

About the Author

Susan Ashley has written over eighteen books for children, including two picture books about dogs, *Puppy Love* and *When I'm Happy, I Smile*. She enjoys animals and writing about them. Susan lives in Wisconsin with her husband and two frisky felines.